FLEX-ABILITY HOLIDAY

Solo-Duet-Trio-Quartet With Optional Accompaniment

SONGS FOR CHRISTMAS, CHANUKAH, AND NEW YEAR'S EVE

Arranged by VICTOR LÓPEZ

D0841807

CONTENTS

(0690B) OBOE/GUITAR (MELODY)/PIANO/
   GUITAR CHORDS/ELECTRIC BASS
(0691B) FLUTE
(0692B) CLARINET/BASS CLARINET
(0693B) ALTO SAX/BARITONE SAX
(0694B) TENOR SAX
(0695B) TRUMPET/BARITONE T.C.
(0696B) HORN IN F

(0697B) TROMBONE/BARITONE/BASSOON/TUBA
(0698B) VIOLIN
(0699B) VIOLA
(0700B) CELLO/BASS
(0701B) PERCUSSION (MALLET SOLO, MALLET HARMONY,
   AUXILIARY PERCUSSION, DRUM SET (SNARE, BASS, CYMBALS))
(0702B) CD ACCOMPANIMENT

Alfred Music Publishing Co., Inc.
P.O. Box 10003
Van Nuys, CA 91410-0003
alfred.com

Project Manager/Editor: Thom Proctor
Cover Design: Ernesto Ebanks and Candy Woolley
CD MIDI Sequencing: Mike Lewis

JINGLE BELLS

C FLUTE

TRADITIONAL
Arranged by VICTOR LOPEZ

Bright rock ♩ = 138

0691B

SANTA CLAUS IS COMIN' TO TOWN

Words by HAVEN GILLESPIE
Music by J. FRED COOTS
Arranged by VICTOR LOPEZ

6

HAVE YOURSELF A
MERRY LITTLE CHRISTMAS

Words and Music by
HUGH MARTIN and RALPH BLANE
Arranged by VICTOR LOPEZ

(I'm Gettin') NUTTIN' FOR CHRISTMAS

Words and Music by
SID TEPPER and ROY C. BENNETT
Arranged by VICTOR LOPEZ

FROSTY THE SNOWMAN

Words and Music by
STEVE NELSON and
JACK ROLLINS
Arranged by VICTOR LOPEZ

0691B

I'LL BE HOME FOR CHRISTMAS

Words by KIM GANNON
Music by WALTER KENT
Arranged by VICTOR LOPEZ

ANGELS WE HAVE HEARD ON HIGH

TRADITIONAL
Arranged by VICTOR LOPEZ

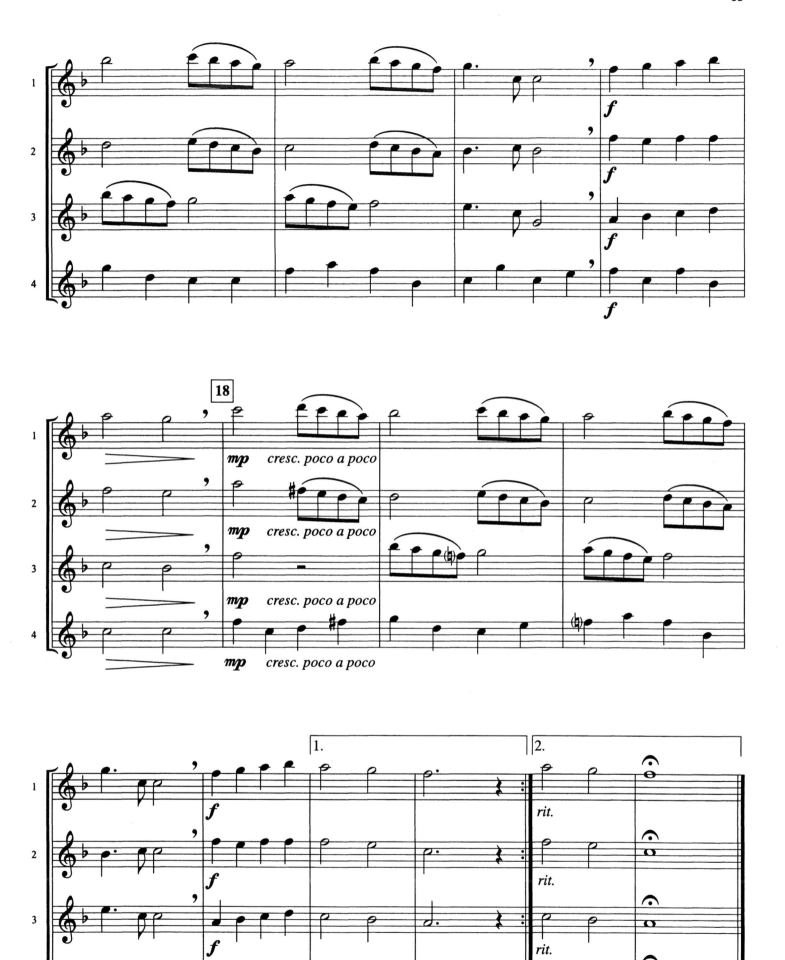

JOY TO THE WORLD

TRADITIONAL
Arranged by VICTOR LOPEZ

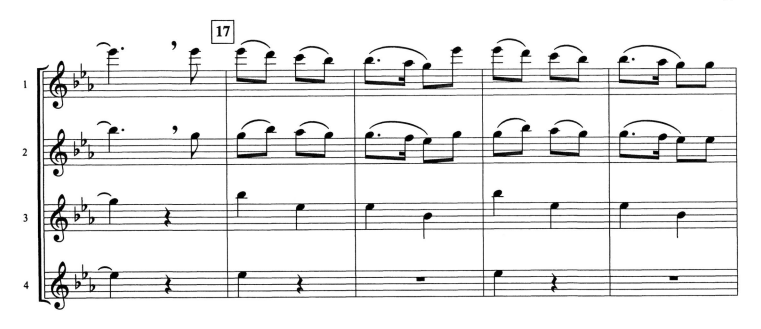

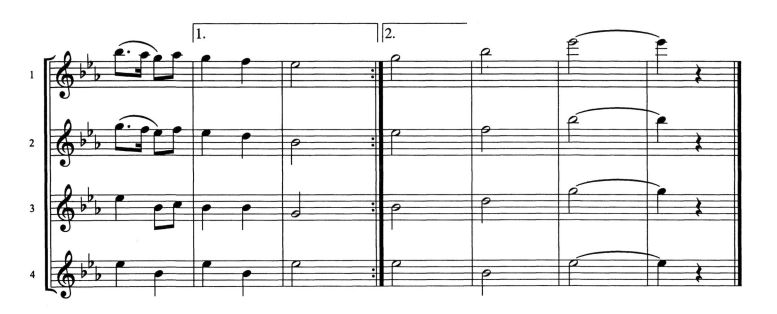

WE WISH YOU A MERRY CHRISTMAS

TRADITIONAL
Arranged by VICTOR LOPEZ

AULD LANG SYNE

TRADITIONAL
Arranged by VICTOR LOPEZ

0691B

CHANUKAH /I HAVE A LITTLE DREYDL

TRADITIONAL
Arranged by VICTOR LOPEZ

FLEX-ABILITY SERIES

Solo-duet-trio-quartet or any small or large ensemble
Woodwinds, brass, strings, percussion

You can play together in harmony with classmates, family, and friends, with any combination of instruments, from less than one year of lessons to two, three, or more years of playing ability. Everybody can play!

Top line	Melody	Level 2½ to 3	Intermediate-level range; sixteenth-note combinations; rock/jazz syncopations
Second line	Harmony	Level 2 to 2½	Wider range; up to sixteenth notes; easy syncopations
Third line	Harmony	Level 1½	Limited range; up to eighth notes
Bottom line	Harmony or bass line	Level 1	Narrow range; whole, half, and quarter notes; easy key and time signatures

The CD accompaniment is available separately. Each song has two tracks: one with a full demonstration performance and one with just the rhythm section for you to play along as a solo, duet, trio, quartet, or larger ensemble.

AD1044

Arranged by Victor Lopez

TITLES:
La Bamba
When the Saints Go Marching In
Eye of the Tiger
Peter Gunn
In the Midnight Hour
China Grove
Jeepers Creepers
Soul Man
Sweet Georgia Brown
Frosty the Snowman
Celebration

INSTRUMENTATION:
(0621B) OBOE/GUITAR/PIANO/BASS
(0622B) FLUTE
(0623B) CLARINET/BASS CLARINET
(0624B) ALTO SAX/BARITONE SAX
(0625B) TENOR SAX
(0626B) TRUMPET/BARITONE T.C.
(0627B) HORN IN F
(0628B) TROMBONE/BARITONE/BASSOON/TUBA
(0629B) VIOLIN
(0630B) VIOLA
(0631B) CELLO/BASS
(0632B) PERCUSSION
(0638B) CD ACCOMPANIMENT